MAEVE BENNETT

HOW TO MANAGE CONTENT

The Ultimate Guide to Successful Content Marketing, Learn the Tricks on How to Create and Distribute Content That is Guaranteed to Build an Audience

Descrierea CIP a Bibliotecii Naţionale a României
MAEVE BENNETT
   HOW TO MANAGE CONTENT. The Ultimate Guide to Successful Content Marketing, Learn the Tricks on How to Create and Distribute Content That is Guaranteed to Build an **Audience** / Maeve Bennett – Bucharest: Editura My Ebook, 2021
   ISBN

MAEVE BENNETT

HOW TO MANAGE CONTENT

The Ultimate Guide to Successful Content Marketing, Learn the Tricks on How to Create and Distribute Content That is Guaranteed to Build an Audience

My Ebook Publishing House
Bucharest, 2021

TABLE OF CONTENTS

INTRODUCTION

As a business owner, you know that how your market your business is at the heart of your success. In fact, most aspects of your business are dependent on you developing a successful marketing campaign. You may provide the best services or sell the best products, but if you don't have a solid marketing plan, potential customers would never know about it.

Today's prospects are looking for useful information, but have a strong resistance to the "hard sell." Most consumers spend the time to research services online before making a purchase. They take the time to study different products, compare prices and features before ever stepping foot in a store. They want good content that helps them make a decision but don't like being sold. In fact, 70-percent of consumers would rather learn about a company through an excellent article rather than advertising.

Compelling content can help your business build strong customer relationships without resorting to the less productive "hard sell" tactics. The content you produce showcases your expertise, which gains consumer trust by highlighting important topics that affect consumers. Well-crafted content can bring traffic to your website and social media accounts, boost your performance on search results pages, and give your audience the chance to share your content with their friends, resulting in higher conversion rates for your business.

Chapter 1

Developing Your Content Marketing Strategy

One of the most powerful arms you can add to your overall marketing strategy is content marketing. Content marketing is used to establish you as a subject matter expert, which leads to an increase in your company's revenue, as well as having a high- profit potential. However, creating content to build your audience and create a successful business is not a fast growth strategy. It takes months for the content you produce to grow into its potential.

Before you begin creating content for your business, you need to have a clear picture of your business goals if you want to develop a successful marketing strategy. This is especially true when it comes to content marketing. It is essential for you to have a consistent approach when it comes to the content that you are producing. Having a regular strategy provides you with content that keeps your audience engaged, resulting in them seeing you as an authority on the subject. When your business is seen as an authority on a subject, your audience is more likely to purchase from you when the time is right.

For your business to see a return on investment regarding your content marketing effort, it is essential that you develop a comprehensive ecosystem around your central content platform. Developing a complete system helps to leverage your resources to help you grow your business, rather than wasting your resources. For you to have a successful content marketing campaign, it is vital that you see your complete content marketing strategy as an ecosystem in which your content is a dynamic medium, where your customers are involved at every stage.

The Content Marketing Ecosystem

The content strategy that you first develop will grow and evolve. For your strategy to be healthy and productive, you must include many different elements. There are two main types of content that you will have to consider when developing your strategy; recurring content and content assets. Recurring content is content that   builds your customer base over time, while content assets are   used as a near-term client acquisition tool.

When working with a recurring system, there are six parts that need to be included to ensure a healthy ecosystem;

- High-quality front-end content

- An opt-in offer

- An email onboarding sequence

- An initial conversion opportunity

- A follow-up sequence

- Another conversion opportunity

The asset system consists of four parts and can be used on its own or combined with the recurring system. The four elements necessary for the asset content system to be useful are as follows;

- A high-quality long-form content asset

- An initial engagement opportunity

- An initial conversion opportunity

- A follow-up email sequence

Here is a quick look at the parts that you should include for both the recurring content system and the content asset system.

The Six Parts of the Recurring Content Ecosystem

High-Quality Front End Content

While this might seem obvious, all of the content that you create for your company must be high quality. It needs to be interesting, informative, and actionable. You want your content to serve a clear purpose for you and your customers. It is vital that you correctly format the content and thoroughly spell-check it before publishing it online. Set up a regular schedule for posting your content and provide the best information on your industry on a consistent basis.

Provide an Opt-In Offer

Publishing content on a regular basis will bring traffic to your site. However, once the visitors are done with the material, they will leave again. An opt-in offer will capture that traffic, so you can continue to market to them once they leave your site. Opt-in offers usually come in the form of a pop-up or a form on the site that will provide an asset in exchange for an email address. Good opt-in offers will include industry reports, white papers, cheat sheets, educational courses, checklists, coupons, webinars, video courses, or demos/downloads.

An Email Onboarding Sequence

After capturing a lead with your opt-in offer, you will need to onboard them with a sequence of automated emails. This usually consists of four to eight emails that educate the subscriber about your company, shares some of your company's best resources, and encourages them to connect with you. This part of the ecosystem engages them on a more individual level and increases their investment in your brand, as well as setting their expectations for their future interactions with your company.

An Initial Conversion Opportunity

After nurturing your leads through your email sequence and providing them with valuable information and generously sharing your expertise, it's time to extend an offer. Your previous interactions should have naturally led to this point so that the subscriber is comfortable with the proposal and be willing to take you up on it.

A Follow-up Sequence

Your initial offer will result in two groups being formed: those who converted and those you did not. It is important to follow-up with both groups. When following up with those who did take you up on your offer you need to a) offer them an upsell or upgrade and b) on-boarded to make the most of what they've purchased. For those who were not converted you should a) offer them a down sell or 'light' version of your original offer to try and get a conversion, and b) put them into a new sequence that will provide them with further value and education to prepare them for your next offer.

Another Conversion Opportunity

Over the course of your relationship with each customer, you'll ideally want to make multiple offers. It is much easier to get a repeat customer than a new one. This means you want to build numerous in-systems that allow you to maximize the value of each customer. Whether you set up an automated email sequence or launch new cycles, it is imperative you have a recurring sales system in place.

The Four Parts of the Asset Ecosystem

A High-Quality Long-Form Content Asset

Books, webinar series, web summits, and multi-part video courses are all considered content assets. For a majority of businesses, books are ideal, because the physical copy can be used as real-world calling cards. They can be sent to potential customers and leverage them into more significant opportunities for your business. This can include interviews and speaking engagements.

An Initial Engagement Opportunity

This part of the ecosystem entails sending an invitation to your prospects to connect with you on a call, participate in an event or webinar, or receive a demo of your product. You need to include a specific next step for the prospect once they've become engaged with your asset that creates for them a real-time or one-on-one interaction with you.

An Initial Conversion Opportunity

The initial conversion opportunity is simply making an offer during the initial engagement with the prospect. Whether you're talking on a demo or webinar or talking to them on the phone, you need to use the moment to invite them to take action on a specific offer.

A Follow-Up Email Sequence

Like in the recurring ecosystem, the follow-up email sequence will divide the prospects into two groups: those who do not convert and those who do. Again, you will need to follow-up with both groups. Through one email sequence, you will onboard your new customers and upsell them on your products, while the other series will be down sold and placed into a different sequence, making them more amenable to your next offer.

It's critical that you have a specific guiding principle for all your company's marketing efforts. The principle will ultimately be what guides your decisions and keeps you focused on the right things. All of your content, whether you are producing content assets or recurring content, needs to be focused on the five pillars discussed in Chapter 3.

Chapter 2

Finding Your Audience

All successful copywriting campaigns contain three elements. First, you need to find the right target audience. Once you've determined your target audience, you need to develop the right offer, and finally, you need the right copy. All three elements must be present if you want your content marketing campaign to be successful. You can hire the best copywriter, but if you aren't targeting the right audience or have a mediocre offer, the work you do on your content will count for nothing.

To create a successful content marketing strategy, you have to have a deep understanding of your audience. You need to focus your efforts on evergreen content that holds its value over time, and that continues to be useful to your audience. While you may have a rough idea of who your target audience is, you probably don't have a clearly defined persona that you can build a marketing strategy around. That's why it is essential for your business to develop a customer avatar.

Why You Need a Customer Avatar

Over the last several years, the concept of a customer avatar has been gaining momentum. Developing a customer avatar allows you to develop a deeper understanding of your customer's motivations, desires, fears, and problems that influence their buying decisions. Creating a profile that indicates your customer's priorities, challenges, and goals, allows you to tailor your marketing campaign to serve them best.

While every business caters to a wide range of customers, creating a customer avatar allows you to identify your primary customer, those individuals for whom your service is a no-brainer. When determining if a market segment is the right fit for your business, you need to take a three-fold approach and consider; perspective, capabilities, and profit potential.

Assessing Perspective

This is about ensuring that your customer's attitudes are in alignment with yours. You are trying to ensure that they have comparable sensibilities, priorities, and direction to your company. It is essential that the perspectives between your customers and your business are in alignment.

Assessing Capabilities

This is about your company's embedded resources. This includes the resources and assets that position your company to serve a specific type of customer better than another. The key to choosing the right audience is determining if your capabilities fit with the perspective and profit potential.

Assessing Profit Potential

When assessing the profit potential of your chosen market, you have to ask yourself the following questions:

- Does your audience have budgets that will accommodate your prices?

- Is your service going to bring them a significant return, making it a no-brainer to do business with you?

- Do you need to add other products or services to increase your profit margins?

Assessing these three areas will provide you with the conceptual framework for the kind of audience you are looking to attract. Now you can begin building a specific customer avatar to represent your target audience. When creating your customer avatar, you need to determine the following.

- Age
- Gender
- Income
- Family status
- Location
- What they desire
- What they aspire to
- Fears
- Frustrations
- Challenges
- Likes
- Dislikes
- What they read
- Their social media habits
- How they relax

Chapter 3

Making the Right Offers

After you've determined who your target audience is, the next step in your content marketing plan is to ensure that you are making the right offers. The products and services that you are offering should be tailored to attract your primary customers. Your primary customers are what matter most and now that you've spent the time to identify them, it is now time to give them what they want.

To understand the kinds of offers that are more likely to be successful in your market, you have to go back and take a look at your primary customers. You must understand what they need, what their problems are, and their motivations in order to find the best offers to offer them. There is a degree of trial and error involved when developing the best offers and it can take some time for the perfect offer to materialize. You might come up with multiple offers that will serve your target audience. To find the right offer you need to have a deep understanding of what matters most to your primary customers. To pinpoint the most valuable thing to offer them, you have to have a deep understanding of your target audience.

Developing the Right Offer

Product development requires a lot of patience, whether you are developing a digital course, physical product, or consulting service. One of the most important things that you can do for your business is developing the right products. Your company is built on what you can offer your customers and simply throwing something together for the sake of having something to sell, is not the right way to grow your business. This makes market validation a critical part of developing the right offers for your target audience. Before you start designing your offering, it is essential to take the following key steps.

Get the Facts

While you might already have a pretty good idea about the problems your customers are facing and the solutions they are looking for, you still need to listen to your customers in order to clarify your offer. You can accomplish this in a number of different ways. You can start by surveying them and asking questions that will help you quickly determine if your assumptions are right. This will also help you decide whether they are using your product or service in the way you think they are and what it is doing for them.

To find out whether your beliefs about your customers are correct, you can ask them the following questions.

- Why did you choose to use the product or service?

- How are you using the product or service?

- What is the key problem that it solves for you?

- What are some secondary problems it solves for you?

- Has it made your life easier? How?

- What do you like best about it? Is there anything you would change?

- Did you consider other solutions? What made you choose our solution?

- Did you have any doubts or concerns? Did you have any questions that weren't addressed?

- Is there anything else you think we should be doing?

If you're a new company and don't have a customer base yet, you can always talk to people that fit in your primary customer avatar and reframe the questions around a possible service or product that you are thinking about offering.

Simplify

You always want to aim for simplicity. If you are unable to explain what you are offering in two to three sentences, then it is too complicated and will not win the attention of your primary customers. You need to be able to articulate the solution you are providing for their problem immediately. The more complicated something seems, the less likely your customer is going to pay attention. It is human nature to look for the path of least resistance. Humans don't like dealing with things that require a lot of our attention, so err on the side of caution and give your customers simplicity.

Review

Always be reviewing your offers. It's inevitable that your market will change. In order to stay afloat, you'll have to keep up with those changes. One of the most damaging things you can do to your business is to adopt a "set and forget" mentality.

You must always remember that your work is not done the moment you settle on a product and your audience. There are a number of things that can change what your target audience wants and needs, so it is imperative that you review your offers on a regular basis.

Small changes in your business can be as powerful as large ones. You need to regularly take stock of your market and what you offer in order to identify these changes. While it can be difficult to be objective about your business, listening to what your customers are saying is key to the health of your business.

Chapter 4

Creating Your Content

Once you've found your audience, decided on your offer and messaging, it's time to start working on your actual content. Before you begin, you need to develop a channel plan to clearly define where you will publish the content once it is complete. Your plan should include the platforms you will use to tell your story, your criteria, process, and objectives for each piece of content you create. You also need to include how you will connect each piece of content to develop a cohesive brand conversation.

When you're ready to start creating your content, you need to keep in mind that everything you create for your company needs to be focused on the following five pillars.

The Five Pillars of Content Creation

Simplicity

The level of complexity will make or break how a piece of content will perform. If you are not able to boil down the topic into something that is easy and simple to digest, then the topic shouldn't be used. While there are some concepts that are complex and those that require an in-depth analysis and technical exploration, you need to strive to address those topics in a simple manner. This is the only way to ensure your audience will come back to your content again.

Specificity

Specificity is closely related to simplicity in that your content creates a self-selecting audience. If done correctly, your audience will continue to come back to your site for your specific solutions. When creating your content, you have to ask yourself the following questions.

- Who is reading the content?

- What is the specific problem they are trying to solve?

- What is the higher order consequence they are trying to achieve?

- What is the precise solution you can provide that helps them achieve this outcome?

Serendipity

Sometimes topics will fall into your lap, and you have to be prepared to grab them immediately. While it is essential to have an editorial schedule, you also need to be flexible enough to change it quickly if something happens. You may get the chance to interview someone amazing and can publish the interview before your competition has the opportunity, or your company might get featured somewhere, giving you the chance to push the momentum as far as you can. It is important to realize that these kinds of opportunities come up all the time. It is essential to pay attention to what is happening around you and capitalize on those opportunities, not allowing serendipity pass you by.

Discipline

When you're putting in the work, serendipity has a way of appearing more often. Being disciplined about producing high-quality content, provides you with the high-quality opportunities your business needs to succeed. The most significant problem many business owners face is finding the time to create the content. Your content will only work when you're consistent. It is imperative that you are publishing on a regular schedule in order to reap the full benefits of your content marketing strategy. If you can't commit to the discipline of doing it yourself, you must find someone else to handle it for you.

If you chose to write the content yourself, you have to pick ideas that inspire you. This is important because it won't matter if you are the most disciplined person in the world, if you find the content boring, you won't want to write about it. Only exciting ideas will energize you enough to be disciplined to maintain your production schedule.

Content Delegation

Having the discipline to do the work, doesn't necessarily mean that you have to do everything yourself. As the leader of your company, creating content may not be the best use of your time, even if you can find themes that excite you. Hiring someone who can help you with creating the content is a high leverage point that you can create. This is especially true if you hire someone that has a writing background.

Creating Recurring Content

The recurring content you create, like blogging, YouTube videos, and podcasts, are what most people think of as content marketing. Unfortunately, many business owners mistake publishing content for marketing. Publishing a lot of content won't guarantee that you will make money. Without a plan that includes collecting emails, sending out onboarding or follow-up content, and sending targeted sales offers you will never gain a loyal following or make money. For you to convert people, you have to make sales offers, no matter what kind of marketing you are doing.

When it comes to producing recurring content, you want to figure out how you can achieve your goals while keeping you motivated to continue creating content on a regular basis. To develop a marketing strategy that will serve your business, you need to ask yourself the following questions.

- What is the purpose of our marketing?
- Who is the audience we are trying to reach?

- What types of marketing should we use? Is content the right fit for our business?

- Is there someone in the company that can produce the content?

- What should our content focus on?

- Is our audience interested in consuming that type of content?

- What other kinds of marketing should we implement to make our content perform for us?

- How will we measure the success of our content marketing strategy?

To create recurring content that will grab the attention of your market, while leveraging that attention into real sales conversions, you have to create the opportunity for conversion. The material that you publish needs to create a situation where your audience has an opportunity to convert on an offer they received early on in the relationship, can convert again at a higher price point down the road, and can refer people to your business that will also convert.

Choosing Your Front-End Content Themes

Content tends to perform best when it is published on a regular basis. Many businesses find producing once a week is enough, while others, who are utilizing social media, find producing several posts every day works for them. However, a lot of businesses struggle to publish on a consistent basis because they don't know what topics they should tackle. This can be extremely discouraging because not only have you wasted your time and missed a valuable marketing opportunity, by you've also failed to deliver to your audience, which will damage your credibility.

One way to avoid falling into this trap is to read through all of your customer service tickets and revisit your conversations with your prospects. Determine the most common questions that are being asked and the topics that you continually have to explain. Also, think about what it is you want to be known for, what your customers want from you, and determine your unique sales proposition. With this information, you can come up with three to four broad themes that you can revisit time and again from different perspectives.

Each of these themes, you can develop numerous subtopics to write about in your weekly content. Sit down at the beginning of each quarter and determine three to four subtopics that you can create content for under the central themes you previously identified. Take some time to come up with a couple of potential headlines for each topic, along with four to five key points to address for each post. Create a spreadsheet and include this information along with a tentative publishing schedule.

This will allow you to sit down and produce quality content each week easily. Having a plan is the easiest way to get it done because you don't have to waste time deciding on a topic, coming up with talking points or battling writer's block. You've already completed the hardest part.

Along with coming up with a handful of regular themes, you will also want to make a list of occasional topics, that you can touch on every once in a while. Plan on covering each of your central themes once a month, and one of your occasional topics every six weeks. Doing this will establish you as an authority on the subject.

Build an Opt-In Offer

Content on its own isn't enough. To build a relationship with your visitors, you have to find a way to continue communicating with them on a regular basis. You can't assume that your customers will remember to check your blog or buy from you unprompted.

In today's information-rich world, it's hard for people to judge what's right and useful. Today's consumers are desperate for transparency and trust in their relationships, including their business relationships. Your content, when paired with the ongoing communication with your customer provides you with the best opportunity to give people both the trust and transparency they desire.

Most of the content that you will be delivering will be distributed on platforms that you don't own, like Facebook, Twitter, search engines, and content networks. These platforms own the traffic, and if they change the way they do business, you have the potential to lose your audience. This is why building a contact list that you own is critical. This is where your opt-in offers will come into play.

Whenever a new contact visits your site, there should be an opportunity for them to join your mailing list for an incentive. Obtaining their email address or getting them to set up an account is imperative for you to build their profile, communicate with them, and create carefully targeted sales offer to send to them when the timing is right.

The opt-in offers you provide don't have to be complicated. Once you have an excellent piece, that contains useful information, don't wait to publish it. For every day that you don't have an active opt-in offer is a day that you are losing valuable leads and wasting your time. While you ideally want to provide your subscribers with a piece of premium content, at the very least you need to have a pop-up box that asks them for their email address.

Build an Onboarding Sequence

Getting someone to provide you with their email address or getting them to create an account with your company is a big win. This micro-commitment is the first step towards having them purchase something from you, and getting their permission to market directly to them. This is a huge deal, and you will want to capitalize on the opportunity.

An email onboarding sequence is used to create a window for you to market directly to your potential customers. Most onboarding sequences consist of four to eight emails that educate your subscribers about your brand, allow you to be engaged with your online community, and that are indoctrinated with your values.

The goal of the sequence is to establish yourself as an authority on the subject matter they opted in to hear about and to get them to take the next step.

No matter what your next contact with the potential customer is, it is mission critical for you to make sure that you are positioning the subscriber to engage with you. You never want to assume that   the prospect will read all the information you provide them and   then decide to get in touch with your or make a purchase. You need to make sure you have something specific you are leading your subscribers toward. It is essential that your subscribers are never unclear about what they should do next. This is true at any point during the cycle as the subscriber moves through your ecosystem, but is particularly true at this stage.

Everything you produce at this point in your content marketing strategy should be driving the prospect toward a real-time interaction with you. You should always be pushing the prospects toward some sort of communication with your company. A critical aspect of high-converting content is that there is always a clear call to action that moves your potential customer through your sales funnel.

Make Sales Offers

To create content that converts, you have to have a conversion moment. In spite of all the progress that has been made in marketing, you still have to make a sales offer in order to convert your prospective customers. There is no possible way for you to extract a sale without first creating a sales offer.

All businesses depend on the number of sales they make. How good your system is, doesn't matter, neither does having a great team, if you don't make a sales offer, you won't complete any sales. You have to be committed to making the sale, which means you have to be able to ignore the fear of rejection, your anxiety about upsetting people, and the voice in your head that said you can't do it.

Sales offers come in all shapes and sizes. Whatever your offer is, it is important that you explicitly offer to give your customer your product or service in return for a specific dollar amount. If you are scared of making sales offers off the back of your content, or you make a half-hearted attempt at a sale without showing the customer the benefits, your content will never covert a single customer, wasting your resources and time, ultimately leading to the failure of your business.

One of the great things about the content ecosystem is that a majority of the people you connect with will be pre-qualified as a potential customer, so they are more likely to have a positive response to your offer.

Follow-up with Your Prospects

It is rare that you will get a conversion the first time you make contact with your prospect. However, if your initial onboarding funnel does its job of bringing them into your business and demonstrating your value, you might have a reasonably high conversion rate from the start. Unfortunately, for most companies, getting the conversion can take a few interactions.

Today, people are more concerned with getting to know that you're a trustworthy and legitimate business and that there are others who have successfully worked with you. If your prospects have gone through each part of the ecosystem, they should know, like, and trust you, and understand how they can benefit from what you are offering. If you haven't converted them, then you have to bring the follow-up system to life.

If you aren't able to convert them from a prospect to a customer in your first interaction, you need to follow-up with them in a couple of weeks. It is important that you follow-up with them as promised and restate their exact motivation for speaking with you, highlighting how you can help them. Be ready to answer any more questions that they might have, and speak directly to the issues that they've already shared with you while reinforcing why you are a great fit. Until someone specifically says they don't want what you are offering and don't want to talk to you anymore, you need to continue to follow-up with them.

Creating Your Content Assets

To demonstrate that you are an authority and that you have an uncommon depth of knowledge in your industry, you should be building content assets. Content assets are long-form pieces of content that can be used to attract the high-end clients. A powerful way to get your company in front of big clients is by sharing your expertise in a generous and transparent way.

Building a strategy around content assets will not work for all businesses. For example, e-commerce companies would be better served developing their content marketing strategy around recurring content. This is the same for businesses that have low price-point products. However, businesses that sell high-ticket items or services will benefit from creating a strategy around content assets because they are a convincing demonstration of authority and credibility.

Content assets should be used to upgrade your recurring content. Unlike recurring content, that gets you in front of a wide audience, content assets put you above the rest of the businesses in your market. It shows that you are serious about your industry, that you are an authority with real expertise and resources while functioning as a calling card, and setting your business apart from the competition.

Clarify Your Concept

The first step in creating content assets is clarifying your concept. Regardless of whether you decide to produce the content yourself or outsource it to a professional, you need to have a clear concept in mind.

Build an Outline

Once you've determined your topic, you will need to build an outline that details what you want to talk about. The foundation of creating a content asset is a robust outline that addresses all the elements that are needed for a customer to convert. This is your roadmap for the entire creation process.

Building a detailed outline of your content will ensure you have included all the important information needed, without having to worry that you've missed something. It allows you to see where you are at all times of the creation process, how much is left to complete, and where things need to be rearranged to make the most sense for the reader.

Building Out the Content

After you've completed building your outline, you'll want to record yourself talking through each and every point that you have listed. Limit each session to no more than an hour, to avoid becoming overly tired, which could lead to a decrease in motivation. When you've completed hashing out all the points in your outline, it's time to start transcribing the information and adding extra resources and context as needed. This system allows you to record all your unique insight, expertise, and perspective without an extensive time commitment.

Once you've transcribed all of the recordings, it's time to focus on the editing process. See if you can find two or three people, that are familiar with the content, and ask them to read over the material. Have them look for typos and grammatical errors along with structural issues, like missing information. Give them a couple of weeks to get through the material, then go through it and implement any edits and suggestions that you believe are appropriate when compared to the original concept of the content.

Leveraging the Asset

This is the process of creating excitement around the asset you've created and building a following with your target audience. You'll want to start marketing the asset while it is being created.

You don't want to wait until its finished to start promoting it to your potential customers. Use this time to line up guest posts, giveaways, podcast interviews, and launch events to build up the launch date.

A Word on SEO

A sound SEO strategy is crucial if you want your content efforts to rank well in search engines. The higher your content ranks, the easier it is to be found by the right audience. When thinking about SEO, there are three rules that you need to keep in mind.

- Search engines want to answer people's questions and make money in the process.

- Search engines know more about how they work than any SEO expert

- Search engines will fix any ranking trick and may penalize you for using it.

When creating SEO content, it is essential to have a primary keyword phrase in mind while writing and it is critical to use the keyword phrase several times throughout the content. When deciding on your primary keywords, you want to aim for ones that have a monthly search volume of less than 10,000 and ones that have low competition. You can find these figures through the Google Keyword Planner tool within Google AdWords.

As you begin creating your content, you want to keep in mind these five guiding principles for creating SEO-friendly content.

- Answer the question

- Provide the best answer to the question

- Provide a complete answer to the question

- Make it actionable

- Over-deliver

SEO is a proven way of increasing your business' ranking when potential customers search for specific keywords. For your content to be successful, it takes more than merely filling your website with keywords; you have to integrate it into your overall content marketing strategy.

Chapter 5

Distributing Your Content

Creating a content marketing strategy that converts is heavily reliant upon having a steady stream of fresh eyes seeing your content. Whether you have implemented a recurring plan or an asset-driven one, you'll never make a cent if no one sees it, no matter how incredible the content. If you want people to engage with your content, you have to be proactive in its distribution.

Email Marketing

Email marketing is still one of the most powerful strategies you can use to get the most out of your content. It is always the most direct way for businesses to connect with their audience. It's the only distribution channel that is sent directly to them and the only one that is personalized down to their name, specific interests, and past purchases.

There are three types of email campaigns that you can use in your business, the welcome campaign, lead nurture campaign, and the offers campaign. Each campaign serves a specific purpose. The welcome campaign is designed to immediately engage your audience and let them know that you'll be communicating with them. The lead nurture campaign is designed to help your audience find your business and build trust. The offer campaign is used to provide them with relevant, timely sales offers.

Utilizing Social Media

With the popularity of social media networks at an all-time high, it has become an essential tool for businesses to get their content in front of the right audience. As potential customers are already using social media to interact with brands, it's a great way to distribute your content to reach as many people as possible.

Great social media marketing can bring your business remarkable success while creating loyal brand advocates and driving leads and sales.

Every social network has its benefits, communication style and challenges. Knowing which platform will work best for you will depend on the audience you are trying to reach, the kind of content you are creating, and the goals you want to achieve.

Facebook

Facebook remains the premier platform to build personal connections with consumers based on their interests. It has a broad reach and a near-universal appeal which make it an easy to manage addition to your content marketing strategy.

Twitter

Twitter has more than 340 million active users a month, making it the king of the marketing micro-conversation. It has quickly become the top social media platform for consumers who are looking to stay informed and discuss what is happening in their   life at that exact moment. Businesses can use it to extend the reach of their long-form content by tweeting a key takeaway and links to the full article.

YouTube

Videos that are uploaded to YouTube, attract billions of views every day, making this platform the king of video sharing. Videos are universally appealing and emotionally resonant, making them a great way to create unique, immersive, and entertaining experiences to help drive brand awareness and accomplishing other top-of-the-funnel marketing goals.

Instagram

Instagram has taken the content-based micro-conversations that made Twitter a household name and added a visual spin. It is the perfect platform for businesses to capture the authentic moments that bring humanity to their market.

Pinterest

Pinterest has become the world's largest scrapbook that elevates content into an easily cataloged art form. The platform works great for content discovery and has become popular with B2C marketers who are trying to turn window shoppers into informed buyers by sharing their passions.

LinkedIn

LinkedIn has long been recognized as the gold-standard of business-focused networking. When the platform opened it Publisher program, that allowed users to publish their own content, the platform began to emerge as a powerful tool for businesses. Now, businesses use the platform to grow their influence and thought leadership, to support the content they've published on other media outlets, and to share the work opportunities they offer.

Google+

Anyone who has a Google product, whether it is Gmail, drive, or analytics, has access to their own personal Google+ page. This makes the platform a wide-reaching, task-focused alternative to other social media platforms. It is a great way to create brand awareness, sharing in-depth industry insights, and for spreading brand influence.

Utilizing social media to distribute your company's content is a must for businesses today. Each platform has its benefits, and it is up to businesses to figure out which ones will work best for distributing their content to their readers.

CONCLUSION

Creating informative and engaging content for your business can feel confusing and discouraging. When it comes to content marketing, it is imperative to develop a complete and detailed blueprint to ensure that your company will see a substantial return on its marketing investment. Taking the time to create your marketing blueprint will give you the tools your business needs to create and distribute thought-provoking and engaging content to build your audience and grow your business.

Printed by Libri Plureos GmbH in Hamburg,
Germany